TURNING CHAOS INTO DESIRE: MANIFESTING CHANGE

Copyright © 2023 by Orion Myst

All rights reserved. No part of this publication may be reproduced, distributed, or transmitted in any form or by any means, including photocopying, recording, or other electronic or mechanical methods, without the prior written permission of the publisher, except in the case of brief quotations embodied in critical reviews and certain other noncommercial uses permitted by copyright law.

Published by White Sands, LLC

Cover design by Orion Myst

ISBN: 979-8-9887095-5-8

First Edition, 2023

LEGAL DISCLAIMER: This book is intended to be used for educational and entertainment purposes only. It is not intended to serve as professional advice of any kind. The author, illustrator, and publisher specifically disclaim any responsibility for any liability, loss, or risk, personal or otherwise, which is incurred as a consequence, directly or indirectly, of the use and application of any of the contents of this book.

TURNING CHAOS INTO DESIRE
Manifesting Change

Written by Orion Myst

DEDICATION

This book is dedicated with love and appreciation to my family - Wendy, Skylar, and Cameron, who stand as my pillar of strength, source of inspiration, and mirrors of transformation. Your unwavering support, acceptance, and love fuel my strength and spark my creativity.

To Forrest, my distant son, this book carries my longing for reconciliation and my promise of enduring love. May we find our way back to each other, turning the chaos of our past into a shared desire for connection and understanding.

And to the world - in the hopes that these insights inspire change, foster connection, and cultivate a space of love and growth for us all.

With Love,
— Orion Myst

PREFACE

Change is the only constant, and yet, so many of us fight the inevitable, clinging to the predictable and the secure. But what if I told you there's a way, a path through which you can harness the very energy of change? A method to reshape your reality, turning chaos into desire, and manifesting tangible positive change?

That's precisely what this book, *Turning Chaos Into Desire: Manifesting Change*, brings forth. It opens up the esoteric world of Chaos Magick, incorporating philosophies pertaining to the Law of Attraction and tailored personal growth practices as a vehicle for transformation.

In writing this book, I've drawn upon my personal experiences, extensive research, and in-depth interviews with accomplished practitioners of Chaos Magick worldwide. Each chapter presents a rich blend of theory and practical techniques designed to awaken your inner alchemist, empowering you to become an active participant in the creation of your life.

But this book goes beyond being an instructional guide. It's an invitation to question, to challenge, and to redefine societal norms. The contrarian examples illustrated in these pages serve as powerful testimonials of the potential for transformation residing within Chaos Magick.

This work is a distillation of diverse philosophies, centuries-old wisdom, and modern mindset theories.

I've attempted to make the complexity of our minds and the symbolic language of the universe both accessible and engaging. Detailed narrations of manifestation rituals, my own manifestation success stories, and contrarian case studies are interspersed throughout the text to provide specific examples that illuminate the path.

As you read, I urge you to keep an open mind and engage directly with the content. Experiment with the guided visualization exercises. Practice the manifestation rituals. Absorb the wisdom imparted by successful magick practitioners during the interviews. And most importantly, in times of doubt or difficulty, refer to the troubleshooting section to navigate common obstacles.

Remember, transformation is a journey, not a destination. Whether you are a beginner attempting to dip your toes into the mystical realm or a seasoned practitioner of magick, there are insights and experiences within these pages that can serve as fertile ground for your personal growth.

May this book inspire you to embrace the chaos, turn desires into reality, and manifest your highest potential.

Enjoy the journey.

— Orion Myst

Personal experience with Chaos Magick

Embarking on my journey with Chaos Magick, I was initially intimidated by its elusive and often misunderstood reputation. Nevertheless, my curiosity prevailed, and I found myself immersing in this vibrant universe, which respected no law—neither scientific nor mystical—but its own.

My first potent encounter with Chaos Magick occurred during an incident that, at first glance, may seem mundane. I was slated for a crucial business meeting that I had put off for weeks, the outcome of which would potentially change my professional trajectory. Anxiety haunted me—fear of rejection, fear of underperforming.

Recalling the teachings of Chaos Magick, I decided to turn this impending chaos into desire. I established a simple sigil, a symbol that represented my desired outcome—securing the business deal. As I crafted this tangible embodiment of my intent, an unfamiliar tranquility washed over me, turning trepidation into anticipation.

I had positioned myself not as a passive player in fate's merciless hands, but an active participant influencing my destiny. The mechanics of Chaos Magick offered liberation from the debilitating victim mentality, steering me towards empowerment.

I meditated on the sigil, infusing my intent into it. Post-meditation, I went about my day, deliberately forgetting the sigil to allow my subconscious mind to anchor itself in the objective. Much to my surprise, the meeting progressed favorably, culminating in a handshake that sealed the deal. This experience cemented my belief in the dynamic power of Chaos Magick— I had turned the chaos of uncertainty into the concrete desire of success.

This personal experience is merely one from my repertoire of Chaos Magick application. Each successful manifestation fortified my confidence, enabling me to tackle larger challenges and manifest increasingly grandeur desires. While each experience differs in context, the underlying theme remains constant— the conscious metamorphosis of chaos to desire, fear to power, uncertainty to confidence.

Purpose and desired outcomes of the reader

From reading *Turning Chaos Into Desire: Manifesting Change*, what can you, as the reader, hope to gain? What do these pages hold for you—practicality, spiritual illumination, or perhaps a magical odyssey of self-discovery?

At heart, this book is a comprehensive guide, offering a practical approach for harnessing the transformative power of Chaos Magick. It aims to guide readers through their individual journeys of manifestation, igniting the potential to morph chaos into desire. Whether you are grappling with personal hurdles or yearning for a deeper manifestation insight, these pages promise an enriching exploration of self-empowerment.

The primary desired outcomes for readers are:

1. An understanding of Chaos Magick—beyond the myths and misconceptions—and its significant role in manifestation.

2. Practical techniques to incorporate Chaos Magick into daily routines. These methods, underpinned by actionable strategies and visualization exercises, offer a tangible pathway for transforming chaos into constructive energy.

3. An invigorated mindset that challenges societal norms and promotes contrarian thinking. Our unique integration of diverse philosophies encourages readers to question mainstream frameworks, thereby forging their path.

While the book is rooted in the vigorous context of Chaos Magick, I do not shy away from amalgamating other potent philosophies. The Law of Attraction and Growth Mindset, for example, complement significant thematic discussions—broadening your intellectual and spiritual repertoire.

As an added bonus, readers will also gain access to diverse perspectives through interviews with successful magick practitioners. These narratives ground the esoteric principles of Chaos Magick in reality, dispelling any lingering skepticism.

In essence, *Turning Chaos Into Desire: Manifesting Change* serves as a catalyst for personal transformation. As a reader, you traverse a journey of empowerment that gains momentum with each practice of Chaos Magick. The ultimate desired outcome—an invincible spirit that thrives amidst chaos and manifests desires with unwavering intent.

TABLE OF CONTENTS

INTRODUCTION   1
   Overview

CHAPTER 1   11
   Unveiling Chaos: Introduction to Chaos Magick

CHAPTER 2   23
   Sculpting the Self: Personal Transformation through Chaos Magick

CHAPTER 3   35
   The Contrarian Mindset: Rethinking Norms

CHAPTER 4   45
   Empowerment Unveiled: Chaos Magick and Personal Power

CHAPTER 5   55
   Manifestation Mechanics: Using Chaos Magick for Desire Realization

CHAPTER 6   71
   Inspirational Anecdotes: Interviews with Successful Magick practitioners

CHAPTER 7   81
  Winning at Wizardry: Optimizing Use of Chaos-Based Techniques

CHAPTER 8   93
  Future Focus: Sustaining Growth and Manifestation

CHAPTER 9   105
  Envoys of Change: Using Chaos Magick to Impact the World

CHAPTER 10   113
  Wrapping the Wand: Concluding Thoughts

APPENDIX   123
  Additional Reading

AUTHOR BIO   129

INTRODUCTION

Welcome reader, to *Turning Chaos Into Desire: Manifesting Change*, a transformative guide that seeks to empower you with the tools and attitudes necessary to harness the raw energy of Chaos Magick. This book is more than a guide—it is a call to awakening, a resonating catalyst for real and tangible change.

This guide draws consistently from my own life and experiences as well as the insights gleaned from countless interviews with successful Chaos Magick practitioners. It stands alone in its conceptualized amalgamation of diverse philosophies—from Chaos Magick to Law of Attraction to Growth Mindset—that subtly color the book's pages. As such, it navigates seamlessly between practical advice, empowering philosophies, and spiritual profundity.

The aim of this book is threefold. First, it unravels the complex tapestry of Chaos Magick, demystifying its principles and practices to clarify its role in manifestation. Next, it provides an array of practical techniques designed to empower and enable you to incorporate Chaos Magick into your everyday life. Finally, it seeks to instigate a shift in mindset—a challenge to societal norms and mainstream thinking.

You will delve into core principles of Chaos Magick and manifestation that are often overlooked in comparable books. My attempt is to blend story-telling and wisdom to breathe life into Chaos Magick, bridging the gap between ancient principles and modern applicability.

TURNING CHAOS INTO DESIRE

This book, with each annotated reference and inked exercise, has been meticulously crafted in an accessible yet thought-provoking manner. Whether you're a novice in magick or a seasoned practitioner, you'll find insights you can apply, and powerful visualization exercises that evoke vivid imagery, inspired actions, and transformative outcomes.

Every chapter of this book is an expedition unto itself, leading you on a journey of personal growth and spiritual discovery. This guide extends the tools necessary to navigate your own path, offering you the reins of control over your desires and destiny. May it illumine your journey of transforming chaos into desire and serve as a beacon of personal empowerment.

Welcome to the journey of a lifetime. Let's venture together into the terrain of hope, courage, and transformation.

Overview of Chaos Magick and manifestation

To the uninitiated, the term 'Chaos Magick' may seem intimidating—imageries of disarray, randomness, and unpredictability may spring up. However, as you delve deeper, you'll find that there is an inherent order within the chaos, a method to the madness.

Chaos Magick, at its crux, is about using belief as a tool to manipulate reality—a metaphysical approach to molding the objective world to mirror our subjective desires (Hine, 1995). It disrupts traditional paradigms by allowing the practitioner to cherry-pick elements from different systems, cultures, and philosophies to construct a uniquely personal spiritual patchwork. Establishing personal relevance and authenticity is at the very heart of Chaos Magick—a departure from universally accepted dogmas to utterly subjective truths (Carroll, 1987).

Manifestation, on the other hand, is about aligning ourselves with the desired outcomes, not through mere wishful thinking but as a result of choosing the right thoughts, emotions, and actions (Leo, 2008). It's commonly known that the most potent form of manifestation involves visualization—a thoughtful process that requires clear intention, vivid imagery, and unwavering focus to create tangible change.

Combining the two takes the process of manifestation to a whole new level. Chaos Magick provides the flexibility and personalization necessary to navigate the dynamic waters of life, while manifestation provides the direction and intent. In amalgamating the two, we find ourselves with a powerful system of transformation that transcends societal boundaries and allows for radical personal growth (DuQuette, 2003).

Connection between Chaos Magick and personal transformation

Indeed, in every human life, there comes a point where everything seems muddled—a chaotic whirlwind of thoughts, emotions, and circumstances.

TURNING CHAOS INTO DESIRE

Think of Chaos Magick as our personal compass through this upheaval, a conduit to channel this tumult into transformative energy (Hine, 1995).

Chaos Magick thrives on establishing subjective relevance—it is entirely personal and moulds itself around the practitioner, not vice-versa (Carroll, 1987). As Hine beautifully puts it, "*Chaos Magick is fluid, allowing the practitioner to shift paradigms at will*" (Hine, 1995, p.45). This fluidity serves as the backbone of personal transformation—allowing us to transition, change, adapt, and grow with newfound resilience.

Through Chaos Magick's unique approach, we start seeing our self-beliefs as entities that little by little construct our reality—a point shared by mystics and modern psychologists alike (Duhigg, 2016). Once we see this, choosing to believe differently becomes an act of alchemy, transforming our internal chaos into a crucible for personal growth (Carroll, 1987).

By employing Chaos Magick, you're encouraged to tear down long-held structures, beliefs, and biases. No longer are you constricted by societal norms or conformity. You begin to think differently, considering alternative, contrarian perspectives. This intellectual liberation is essential to personal transformation—it fosters an environment ripe for self-reflection, exploration, and growth (DuQuette, 2003).

Remember, Chaos Magick isn't an escape route from chaos but a means to harness it for personal empowerment and transformation. After all, as Friedrich Nietzsche once said, "*One must still have chaos in oneself to be able to give birth to a dancing star.*"

Importance of contrarian thinking in the process

If the conformity of thought is the lock that keeps us bound to our present states, contrarian thinking is the key to liberation, a fact deeply rooted in Chaos Magick and ably demonstrated in the practice of Manifestation (Wilson, 1979). This holistic embrace of challenging the status quo is not merely an act of rebelliousness; it's a conscious commitment to explore, question, and redefine the norms and beliefs we often accept unquestioningly (Hine, 1995).

I will champion contrarian thinking as the catalyst for change. Deviating from the paved pathway of common consensus, and forging one's path might be daunting initially. Still, it is through charting these unfamiliar terrains that we discover the power to manifest change.

The potency of contrarian thinking lies in its inherent freedom—freedom from the echoes of societal mores and freedom to embrace a fresh perspective, one that aligns with the pursuit of personal transformation (Carroll, 1987). How we perceive our reality deeply influences what we manifest (Duhigg, 2016), and contrarian thinking is our compass—guiding us from the labyrinth of pre-established paradigms towards the clarity of individual understanding.

Through the lessons learned in this book, our raw, chaotic thoughts will gradually solidify into focused, directed desires. The energy once scattered aimlessly across multiple realms now has a verdant destination for fruition.

Remember, Chaos Magick is about finding your truth amidst the swirling vortex of chaos (Hine, 1995; Carroll, 1987), and contrarian thinking is your steadfast guide. As they say, the wind doesn't break a tree that bends. So, in the hurricane of societal pressures and stereotypes, be resilient—be unafraid to sway against the wind.

References

- Augustin, S., & Leder, H. (2006). Art in context: Understanding aesthetic diversity. Speakers' Corner.

- Elliot, A. J., & Maier, M. A. (2007). Color and psychological functioning. Current directions in psychological science, 16(5), 250-254.

- Carroll, P. (1987). Liber Null & Psychonaut: An introduction to chaos magic. Weiser Books.

- DuQuette, L. M. (2003). The Magick of Thelema: A handbook of the rituals of Aleister Crowley. Weiser Books.

- Duhigg, C. (2016). Smarter Faster Better: The secrets of productivity in life and business. Random House.

- Hine, P. (1995). Condensed Chaos: An introduction to chaos magic. Original Falcon Press.

- Leo, K. (2008). The Map: Finding the magic and meaning in the story of your life. Hay House.

- Wilson, R. A. (1979). Prometheus Rising. Falcon Press.

CHAPTER 1

Unveiling Chaos: Introduction to Chaos Magick

Step into a realm where reality bows to the power of the mind. This is a space infused with the raw, unfettered essence of Chaos Magick (Hine, 1995). An imposing concept? Perhaps. But I am here to demystify it for you—to siphon off the external commotion and reveal the transformative core.

So, what is Chaos Magick? Simply put, it's less about brewing potions in a cauldron and more about brewing powerful, change-centric thoughts within the mind. Phil Hine (1995), a magick practitioner, defines Chaos Magick as "*an attitude, a philosophical outlook that promotes the pragmatist use of belief as a tool.*" As you illuminate this path of understanding, envision Chaos Magick as a manifestation compass—arising from the chaos within and guiding outward resonance.

Upon this path of enlightenment, the norms that society has etched upon the slate of belief become your first obstacle. Conformity, friends, is the absolute bane of Chaos Magick. To truly ascend into the realms of manifestation, one must embrace contrarian thinking, challenging and discarding those norms that no longer serve our growth (Carroll, 1987). This pivotal shift is the beating heart of the transformation I'm inviting you into.

Critics may brand Chaos Magick as a retreat into fantasy, a weak evasion from the challenges of what we perceive as reality. Contrary to this misinterpretation, the foundation of Chaos Magick is in constant flux—ever-adapting, ever-evolving, like the fluid fluctuations of thought itself. Robert Anton Wilson (1979) elucidates this even further in his seminal work 'Prometheus Rising', in which he refers to Chaos Magick as an art and science at the crossroads of reality and perception, empowering one to shape the material from the immaterial.

In contrast to linearity, Chaos Magick embraces multidimensionality—inspiring you to question, to delve deep, and to shatter the glass ceilings of your limiting beliefs (Duhigg, 2016). As you step past the crossroads, plunging into the spiraling chaos inside, remember the lore of the magick practitioner: to manifest change is to ride the currents of desire, harnessing them with the almighty harness of belief.

As we embark on this enchanting journey with *Turning Chaos Into Desire: Manifesting Change*, we will explore the potent elements of this realm—the creation, the transformation, and the manifestation. These processes, though semi-illusory and shrouded in mystery, are the very arteries that carry lifeblood to your magickal power.

History and basic principles of Chaos Magick

Chaos Magick burst onto the metaphysical scene in the late 20th century, a brainchild of Peter Carroll and Ray Sherwin (Carroll, 1987; Sherwin, 1978). These two transformative thinkers, in a collaborative partnership, pioneered a movement that shattered the metaphorical shackles of traditional magick practices. Emerging from the cauldron of Thee Temple ov Psychick Youth and the Illuminates of Thanateros, Chaos Magick held its roots firmly in the revolutionary Zeitgeist of the 1970s and 1980s (Hine, 1995; Carroll, 1987).

Armed with the primordial understanding that belief wields the power to shape reality, Carroll and Sherwin birthed an eclectic magick system—one that didn't expend efforts in worshipping gods or adhering to rigid systems but thrived on flexibility, individuality, and empowerment (Carroll, 1987).

Diving into its core principles, Chaos Magick endorses the leveraging of personal beliefs as tools for creating wanted changes (Hine, 1995). This central tenet, often encapsulated in Carroll's (1987) famous adage "*Nothing is true, everything is permitted,*" recognized the inherent subjectivity of truth and the limitless potential within the human psyche. It underscored the empowering belief that anything is possible once we remove the constraints of societal conditioning.

It's crucial to note here that Chaos Magick doesn't deny the world's logic, nor does it circumvent the physical laws we encounter daily. Instead, it encourages a shift in perspective—seeing 'reality' as infinitely malleable, guided by the perceptions and beliefs we hold.

As you journey deeper within the expanse of Chaos Magick, you'll encounter the concept of 'gnosis'. This state, a pivotal catalyst in the manifestation process, embodies the undistracted and single-pointed awareness that fuels magickal acts

(Carroll, 1987). Gnosis, attainable via methods like meditation, orgasm, or sensory deprivation, acts as a gateway to the unconscious mind—a conduit channelizing your desire into the etheric realms of manifestation (Carroll, 1987; Hine, 1995).

Enlightening as this retrospective journey sounds, we mustn't lose sight of the path ahead—an uncharted voyage into a realm lit by the luminescent glow of personal transformation and self-mastery. Guiding you along this enchanting path, I encourage you to harness the essence of Chaos Magick—the flexibility of belief, the expansiveness of vision—and integrate them into your journey towards unravelling your latent powers of manifestation.

Role of chaos in the manifestation of desires

Immersed in a world obsessed with order and control, you—an awakened beacon of desire and possibility—have begun your intense explorative journey into Chaos Magick. In this realm of enchantment, your deep-seated yearnings find the freedom to transmute into concrete reality.

Chaos is a force of nature—unruly, spontaneous, and unpredictable. Yet, underneath this seemingly volatile exterior, it serves a cosmic purpose. It's the vigorous shaking of the kaleidoscope of existence, creating beautiful, unexpected patterns (Sherwin, 1978). And it's within this realm of infinite possibilities that your desires begin their transformative journey to manifestation.

Chaos, in its essence, isn't about disorder or destruction. It's about potential. It's about unleashing the vast reservoirs of creative energy concealed within the convention-laden recesses of your mind. It's about challenging the rigid structures, questioning the deeply-embedded beliefs, and reinventing your reality from a place of immense personal power (Carroll, 1987).

Understanding the role of Chaos in manifestation necessitates a leap of faith. It involves releasing control, stepping away from linear-world thinking, and embracing the malleable substance of the universe (Hine, 1995). It involves building a relationship with the unpredictable, recognizing disruption as a gateway to growth, and ultimately aligning your will with the spontaneous rhythmic dance of existence.

Contrary to the popular misconception, chaos is not antithetical to order. Instead, it is an inherent part of the universal order—a mysterious, fluid part that acts as the cosmic womb where unseen desires actualize into tangible reality (Greer, 2003).

Steeped in the principles of Quantum Physics, Chaos Magick asserts that before material outcomes take form, they exist as endless probabilities within the quantum field (Zukav, 1979). It is here that the role of the chaos magician gains significance. As a chaos magician, your task is to perform mind-altering rituals and direct focused intent, thus collapsing the quantum wave into a desired reality (Carroll, 1987).

The realm of Chaos Magick beckons the daring and the imaginative. So, dear Reader, let's delve further into this dimension, dancing amidst paradoxes, communing with randomness, and yet, wielding the potent energy of focused desire to manifest the reality you seek.

Exploring the unseen forces for positive change

As a chartered cosmic passenger of life's journey, it would not be uncommon to sometimes feel overwhelmed by the magnitude of different forces that constantly shape and tread your reality, many of which may appear invisible to you. To use these unseen forces as catalysts of positivity can seem daunting. However, harnessing and directing these forces towards your intention forms the heartfield of Chaos Magick (Carroll, 1987).

The unseen forces we talk about do not constitute a mystical realm inaccessible to human senses. They exist as unbridled potentialities nestled within the moments of everyday existence, within the nucleus of all your interactions and thoughts, and even within the boundaries of your constraints and challenges. Embracing these unseen forces underpins the art of manifestation through Chaos Magick, where the mundane is infused with endless possibilities (Hine, 1995).

Quantum physics reveals that, at its most fundamental level, the entire universe is an enormous field of vibrating energy (Zukav, 1979). This unseen energy field resonates with potential, acting as a canvas upon which your deep-seated desires begin their journey towards actualization. This field, primarily unseen yet ever present, is the force behind the manifestation of everything that you perceive in your tangible reality.

The role of a Chaos magician, therefore, is to sculpt these unseen forces, creating energetic symphonies through rituals of intention, visualization, and resonance. Merely wishing for a specific outcome is not sufficient. The task lies in aligning your mental and emotional vibrations with that of your desired reality, thereby collapsing the myriad probabilities within the quantum field to yield your preferred outcome (Carroll, 1987).

Drawing upon the principles of Chaos Magick, it's not only plausible but also empowering to weave these unseen forces into a cocoon of transformation and growth. You, dear reader, as the master of your destiny, can harness these forces to mold the malleable substance of the universe according to your deepest desires. Doing so, however, requires a shift in perspective, from seeing the unseen as elusive to understanding it as an unlimited reservoir of potential.

References

- Carroll, P. (1987). Liber Null & Psychonaut: An introduction to chaos magic. Weiser Books.

- Duhigg, C. (2016). Smarter Faster Better: The secrets of productivity in life and business. Random House.

- Greer, J.M. (2003). The New Encyclopedia of the Occult. Llewellyn Publications.

- Hine, P. (1995). Condensed Chaos: An introduction to chaos magic. Original Falcon Press.

- Sherwin, R. (1978). The Book of Results. Revelations 23 Press.

- Wilson, R. A. (1979). Prometheus Rising. Falcon Press.

- Zukav, G. (1979). The Dancing Wu Li Masters: An Overview of the New Physics. HarperCollins Publishers.

CHAPTER 2

Sculpting the Self: Personal Transformation through Chaos Magick

Unveiling the powers of Chaos Magick you are introduced to an untamed domain of potentialities, concealed within the randomness and dynamism of life. It's an exploration where the uncertainty of your 'self', rather than obstructing progress, becomes a sign welcoming personal transformation (Hine, 1995).

Within this realm of perpetual change, your self is not a static entity; it is in fact, an evolving sculpture. A work of art continually refined and redefined by your perceptions, your actions, your beliefs, and most significantly your desires. Through the lens of Chaos Magick, the sculpture of your 'self' becomes an eternally moldable mass ripe for conscious crafting.

While embracing chaos and recognizing the mutable nature of the self form the first steps towards personal transformation, the real magick springs from the conscious attempt to mould this change. Magick is neither about defying the physical laws that govern our world nor about mere spell-casting; it's about aligning your deepest desires with the boundless potentiality within the realm of chaos (Carroll, 1987)

Understanding the link between personal transformation and Chaos Magick

Many of us, consciously or unconsciously, are in a perpetual search for self-improvement. We constantly pursue goals, tweak habits, and strive to refine our personalities, all in the hopes of polishing our 'self'. What if I told you Chaos Magick could significantly uplift and expedite this journey? The proposition may seem audacious but stay with me as I unpack the profound link between personal transformation and Chaos Magick.

Before we dive into the mechanics of this linkage, it's essential to understand the core idea behind Chaos Magick itself. Chaos Magick, as derived from the works of Carroll (1987), places chaos or unpredictability at the center of its philosophy. It encourages its practitioners to use their beliefs as tools, to finely tune their thoughts to match the vibrations of their desires, thereby deeply ingraining the images of an improved future self into the chaotic tapestry of the universe.

In essence, Chaos Magick is not merely about wielding external energies, but more significantly about harnessing the internal ones - your thoughts, your emotions, your desires, and your beliefs.

Now, how does all this facilitate personal transformation?

Transformation of the 'self' – the process of redefining who we are, how we behave, what we perceive, lies at the very heart of Chaos Magick. The fascinating aspect of this process, as Hine (1995), explains, is its fluidity. Simply put, there is no finish line to cross or a final form to acquire in personal transformation.

As delightful as it is daunting, this endless potential for metamorphosis paints a liberating picture where one can endlessly continue to evolve, adapt, and improve. Herein lies the empowerment potential of Chaos Magick.

The understanding that 'self' is not static, but an evolving entity that you can consciously sculpt, provides a formidable sense of agency. This idea, when seeped in Chaos Magick, lays the foundation for a transformative journey characterized by autonomy and intentional living.

Now, it's one thing to travel this transformative journey under the whims of random external influences, and a whole other to navigate it with intentionality and direction. And this is where the magick happens. Mastery of Chaos Magick equips you with the tools to become the deliberate architect of your transformation.

As we explore further into this book, we shall delve deeper into these tools, these practices, and routines resiliently born from the chaos: the rituals, the visualizations, the belief matrices, and much more.

You'd be surprised, possibly even daunted, to discover how powerfully your life can be steered by actively channeling chaos to manifest your desires. But that's the beauty of it. That's the promise of Chaos Magick and personal transformation – an exploration loaded with surprises, the evolving masterpiece of the 'self'.

Techniques for self-awareness and introspection

In the grand journey of personal transformation, becoming perceptively aware of your 'self' is the cornerstone. A successful engagement with Chaos Magick relies heavily on this fine-tuned self-awareness, and introspection is your methodology to achieve this (Hoffman, 2016). In this chapter, we'll explore techniques that will deepen your understanding of your inner self, and thus, empower your manifesting prowess.

The first technique is Journaling. It's beautifully simple yet incredibly powerful. You don't need to be a brilliant writer to maintain a journal, just be honest. The magic lies in articulating your thoughts, your feelings, your dreams, and your fears. As you delve more profound into your self-documentation, unforeseen patterns will start to emerge - the subtle triggers for your emotions, the behavioral patterns that dictate your decisions, or the recurrent imagery that fills your dreams. Journaling can shine a blinding light on these otherwise obscure constructs.

Moreover, as you write, you're actually 'talking' to yourself, promoting active self-dialogue (Adams, 1990).

The second technique is Meditation. Not just relaxing the mind, but honestly exploring it. Consider meditation as a deep-sea dive into your consciousness. With every breath, you dip further, observing thoughts as they float by, not interacting, just acknowledging. With practice, you navigate effortlessly through this ocean of thoughts and emotions, gaining clarity and control over your internal realm (Kabat-Zinn, 1990).

The third technique is 'Thought Cataloging'. It's like a mental organization of your thoughts. Consciously notate what you think in different scenarios, what you feel in those particular situations, and how these elements combine to influence your actions. This technique aids you in spotting redundant thoughts and eliminating behavioral redundancies, focusing your energy on desirable thoughts and actions.

These techniques are not one-size-fits-all solutions. Everyone has distinct mental landscapes, unique emotional languages, and specific mental roadmaps. Explore these techniques, and remember, the central aim is to understand not judge, to explore not exploit.

Embrace this journey of self-awareness and introspection. May it illuminate your path to personal transformation and guide you expertly in the incredible chaos of desire manifestation.

Application of Chaos Magick in everyday life for personal growth

Our everyday life is a beautiful amalgamation of ordinary routines, extraordinary moments, envisioned dreams, and unforeseen challenges. The real question lies in how we can manifest our desires, our 'change,' amid these chaotic circumstances. What if I told you that the answer lies in the very chaos itself? That Chaos Magick could be utilized as an empowering tool for your personal growth right in the crucible of your everyday life.

James Shelley, a modern Chaos magick practitioner, rightly quotes, "*You are the magician. Non-judgment, interruption, refinement, the work of chaos, these are yours because they are you*" (Shelley, 2015). The understanding and application of Chaos Magick doesn't call for a grand hidden temple or mystical artifacts. It invites you into your own awareness, into your daily life where the chaos of existence melds with the power of your potential.

Consider Chaos Magick as a vibrant palate that you can customize according to your unique tastes, applying different 'colors' to your routine life. From your morning coffee contemplation to your nighttime dreams, Chaos Magick can enhance each moment with new depth and purpose.

Let's illustrate through a simple, everyday example. Imagine, every day, on your way to work, you pass a beautiful park. You dream about having time to sit and enjoy its beauty but are always rushed. Use Chaos Magick to manifest this desire. Visualize the desired reality, feel the calm and serenity of sitting near that blooming flower bed, bask in the imagined sun's warmth, and soak in the melodious bird tweets. Now, in the heart of this visualized reality, inject your will, your intent to create this experience genuinely (Hine, 1995). This is a simplistic example but serves to demonstrate the subtle and straightforward application of Chaos Magick in your everyday life for manifesting changes.

Applying Chaos Magick in your personal growth journey invokes constant self-awareness, mind-body connections, and emotional intelligence. It demands an active reshaping of your perceptions, values, and beliefs. This might sound daunting, but remember, "*The Secret of change is to focus all of your energy not on fighting the old, but on building the new*" (Millman, 1980). Believe in your power to manifest and let your everyday life become the canvas for the masterpiece of your desired change.

Remember, Chaos Magick is a non-commodity. It's not something that someone else can sell to you; it's something only you can cultivate within yourself.

References

- Adams, K. (1990). Journal to the self: Twenty-two paths to personal growth. Warner Books, Inc.

- Carroll, P. (1987). Liber Null & Psychonaut: An introduction to chaos magic. Weiser Books.

- Hine, P. (1995). Condensed Chaos: An Introduction to Chaos Magic. New Falcon.

- Hoffman, D. (2016). The Art & Science of Mindfulness: Integrating Mindfulness into Psychology and the Helping Professions. American Psychological Association.

- Kabat-Zinn, J. (1990). Full catastrophe living: Using the wisdom of your body and mind to face stress, pain, and illness. Delacorte Press.

- Millman, D. (1980). Way of the Peaceful Warrior: A Book that Changes Lives. HJ Kramer.

- Shelley, J. (2015). Advanced Magick for Beginners. Aeon Books.

TURNING CHAOS INTO DESIRE

CHAPTER 3

The Contrarian Mindset: Rethinking Norms

The world changes, and with it, we too must change. Our societal norms, beliefs and notions are in a constant state of flux. But what if you began to rethink those norms? What if you embraced a contrarian mindset? Welcome to Chapter 3, where we delve into reimagining the world not just as it is, but as we would have it be with the power of Chaos Magick.

A contrarian, by definition, is a person who opposes or rejects popular opinion (Wordnik, n.d.). As your guide along this transformative journey, I invite you to become a contrarian. Not for the sake of being different, but for seeking truth, understanding, and ultimately, personal growth. *"The reasonable man adapts himself to the world: the unreasonable one persists in trying to adapt the world to himself. Therefore, all progress depends on the unreasonable man"* - George Bernard Shaw (1903). So, is our task to become unreasonable? Perhaps.

Throughout history, progress has often been delivered by those brave enough to defy convention. Be it in science, art, or spirituality, contrarians have left their mark on our shifting, evolving norms. Chaos Magick, at its core, embodies this contrarian ethos. It isn't about rejecting societal norms but rather re-examining, questioning, and if required, altering them to truthfully reflect your desired reality.

Let's take a short detour into the world of physics. Niels Bohr and Albert Einstein had an ongoing debate about quantum mechanics' nature. Einstein, a firm believer in deterministic theories, famously stated, "*God does not play dice with the universe*" (Einstein, 1926). Bohr, on the other hand, contended that randomness and uncertainty prevailed at the quantum level. Bohr was the contrarian here; his perspective eventually cemented the concepts of quantum mechanics, proving that sometimes a host of improbable ideas can shape reality.

Similarly, Chaos Magick advocates for a mix of belief systems, shuffling beliefs like a deck of cards, choosing which suit to play at a given moment. It is not determined by any deterministic theories or dogmas. It values personal experience above all else (Hine, 1995). Applying this to personal growth means accepting inconsistent realities, embracing uncertainty, and creating changes.

However, adaptability is not the same as inconsistency. Chaos Magick doesn't promote arbitrary belief shifts. Instead, it invites mindful choice, deliberation, and discernment. It pushes you to question the default and embrace the extraordinary.

Embracing a contrarian mindset does not just mean defying norms for defiance's sake. It's about exploring alternatives, questioning oneself, and holding the courage to change our perspective when needed. As we explore further, the practical techniques of Chaos Magick will help illuminate this process, enabling you to effectively wield this contrarian mindset as a tool for manifesting change in your life.

Practical examples of successful contrarian thought

Challenging the status quo lies at the heart of contrarian thinking. It demands courage, resilience, and the audacity to dream beyond the societal framework. Chaos Magick, with its rebellious spirit, urges us to embrace such a mindset as a stepping stone toward personal growth and manifestation.

Do you recall George Bernard Shaw's wise words about the "*unreasonable man*"? Let's take a closer look at examples who have adopted this approach and turned their dreams into tangible, groundbreaking realities.

Our exploration begins with Galileo Galilei, the heliocentrism proponent whose defiant stand against the established geocentric concept of the universe sparked a scientific revolution (Mosley, 2011). Despite facing the wrath of the Church and enduring house imprisonment, Galilei remained steadfast in his beliefs. His story highlights the intensity of challenges contrarians often encounter; however, his unyielding spirit and eventual validation demonstrate that no barrier is insurmountable when armed with truth.

From the scientific realm to the artistic one, consider Pablo Picasso's innovative artistic style. Rejecting the traditional emphasis on imitating nature, Picasso, along with Georges Braque, pioneered the Cubism movement and transformed painting and sculpture's face. His unique artistic perspective demonstrated the liberating power of a contrarian mindset.

In recent times, the world has witnessed how contrarian leaders in technology, like Steve Jobs and Elon Musk, have altered industry norms and reshaped our lives. Jobs' emphasis on combining elegance with functionality transformed Apple into a global tech giant simultaneously defining and defying industry trends (Isaacson, 2011).

Similarly, Musk's audacious visions of revolutionary transportation systems and interplanetary travel have disrupted multiple industries. His companies, SpaceX and Tesla, exemplify his belief in challenging convention and striving for the extraordinary (Vance, 2015).

These success stories underline the tremendous transformative potential of contrarian thought, aligning closely with our Chaos Magick philosophy. By daring to walk away from the trodden path, these individuals have not only redefined their personal realities but have also shifted societal paradigms.

As we move forward, let's keep these powerful examples in mind, empowering us to manifest our dreams by leveraging the seemingly chaotic forces around us and fueling our contrarian spirit.

Development and cultivation of a contrarian mindset

Harnessing the unseen forces of chaos to manifest desires requires a significant shift in our paradigm - the adoption of a contrarian mentality. This mindset challenges established norms, questions prevailing perspectives and boldly treads unconventional paths (Elder, 2004). What does this imply for practitioners of Chaos Magick?

Firstly, in the grand arena of ideas and beliefs, becoming a contrarian means daring to swim against the current. Do you remember our earlier discussion about Galileo Galilei, the renowned physicist who defied popular beliefs of his time and paved the way for a scientific revolution? By choosing to question and challenge the accepted geocentric model of the universe, he redefined the boundaries of scientific knowledge (Dreyer, 1953).

To foster a contrarian mindset, one must first develop a healthy skepticism. Question assumptions. Analyze facts critically. Don't accept information at face value or adhere strictly to societal norms. Embrace ambiguity and paradoxes. Cultivating this mindset deepens our understanding of the world, facilitating a more active engagement with the Chaos Magick philosophy.

Secondly, the contrarian mindset is at odds with conformity. In a world wrought with conformity pressure, it requires courage to diverge from the norm - to think, act, and be different. From a Chaos Magick standpoint, such non-conformity is essential for personal transformation and growth.

Consider how Steve Jobs shook the tech industry with his radical ideas and relentless pursuit of perfection. Trapped in the 'functional design' norm, the industry overlooked aesthetics. Jobs bucked the trend, focusing on merging elegance with functionality, and in the process, redefined industry standards and amplified Apple's international prowess (Isaacson, 2011).

Lastly, as contrarians in a society constricted by stereotypes and expectations, our greatest challenge – and victory – lies in defying social constructs. Our mission as practitioners of Chaos Magick is to burst the cage of societal norms and soar on the wings of rebellious imagination and relentless determination.

So, dare to defy. Dare to dream. Defy conventions, embrace the unexplored, and rise above mediocrity. When you align yourself with such contrarian energy, you'll discover manifesting desires through Chaos Magick becomes an intuitive, natural pursuit.

References

- Dreyer, J. L. E. (1953). A History of Astronomy from Thales to Kepler. Dover Publications.

- Einstein, A. (1926). Letter to Max Born.

- Elder, L. (2004). The Miniature Guide to Critical Thinking Concepts & Tools. The Foundation for Critical Thinking.

- Hine, P. (1995). Condensed Chaos: An Introduction to Chaos Magic. New Falcon.

- Isaacson, W. (2011). Steve Jobs. Simon & Schuster.

- Mosley, A. (2011). Bearing the Heavens: Tycho Brahe and the Astronomical Community of the Late Sixteenth Century. Cambridge University Press.

- Shaw, G. B. (1903). Man and Superman: A Comedy and a Philosophy. Brentano's.

- Vance, A. (2015). Elon Musk: Tesla, SpaceX, and the Quest for a Fantastic Future. HarperCollins.

- Wordnik. (n.d.). Wordnik dictionary.

CHAPTER 4

Empowerment Unveiled: Chaos Magick and Personal Power

Chaos magick invites us to harness the primitive yet potent energy of chaos. This raw, untamed force, at first glance, appears threatening, a realm of destruction and confusion. But seen through the prism of Chaos Magick, it transfigures into groundwater feeding the roots of personal empowerment (Carroll, 1987).

The empowerment we seek is an affirmation of our ability to shape our reality, a confirmation of control over circumstances that can mushroom from the mundane to the monumental. But how does Chaos Magick play into this?

First, Chaos Magick opens the door to boundless possibilities. Our daily existence, ruled by predictable systems and patterns, underestimates the potential for randomness and novelty. Chaos Magick bucks this trend, revealing a landscape where limitation gives way to liberation.

Think of the classic 'butterfly effect' in chaos theory, where a small input can trigger grand, unforeseen consequences (Lorenz, 1963). This idea parallels our effort in Chaos Magick to manifest grand changes through seemingly simple acts. The ability to spark such significant shifts illuminates the capacity for personal empowerment residing within us.

Secondly, Chaos Magick reminds us that the future is not set in stone. By adapting and improvising, reshaping beliefs, and employing diverse magical techniques, we can sculpt a future that aligns with our deepest aspirations (Sherwin, 1992).

Finally, personal empowerment plants the seed of resilience within us. Life is a wild ride, and Chaos Magick, imbued with wisdom and adaptability, impels us to brave its storms with unshaken resolve.

The concept and importance of personal empowerment

Personal empowerment isn't merely about feeling capable; it is an intimate dance with one's potentiality. It is an acknowledgement of one's potency to curve life's trajectory towards their deepest desires, a consenting marriage with the idea that we are the sculptors of reality, not mere spectators. It whispers the daring truth that you are not tossed by the tumultuous seas of fate but instead are the helmsman charting your course.

TURNING CHAOS INTO DESIRE

Magick gives embodiment to this empowerment (Carroll, 1987). Recognizing this, Chaos Magick takes it a step further and reveals an uncluttered path to realizing your full potential. For in the tumultuous waltzes of chaos, we find the breeding ground for nascent desires, the nursery where intentions crystallize into manifestations.

Harnessing this power requires understanding ourselves at a profound level and recognizing our innate strength, resilience, and co-creative ability. The first step is recognizing the Chaos that resides within us, the swirling vortex of endless possibilities. Next, we learn effective magick strategies to guide this inner power to birth our deepest desires.

Our power of manifestation is like a raw Ammolite gem, opaque and guarded. It's through the refining fires of Chaos Magick that its true colors burst forth. As Chaos Magick practitioners, we wield the chisel and hammer, cracking open the ordinary crust to uncover extraordinary radiance. Once we believe in this power and learn to harness it efficiently, we remain no longer a pawn adrift in life's turbulent sea but become the sculptor of our destiny.

The successful manifestation requires total alignment: mental, emotional, and energetic. It is more than reciting spells or rituals; it is about invoking a potent inner force and directing it into existence. As the ancient Hermetic axiom reminds us, "*As above, so below, as within, so without.*" The outer reflects the inner, the seen mirrors the unseen. Our ability to manifest our desires hinges on our inner alignment, an echo of our outer world (Sherwin, 1992).

Empowerment births resilience and adaptability. Often, life presents us unexpected situations, abrupt changes, or sudden shifts in our carefully drawn plans. By utilizing the teachings of Chaos Magick and our personal powers, we learn to flow with the currents, transforming the unexpected into conduits for our desires.

Chaos Magick techniques for fostering empowerment

In this journey of rediscovery, the idea of personal empowerment finds root-ball and blooms onto the fertile soil of potentiality. Chaos Magick leaves no stone unturned on this trail to self-empowerment.

Embracing the realm of chaos is the first step towards harnessing its potent energy. To engage fully with chaos, one needs to dismantle societal norms and prescribed belief systems. This paradigm shift facilitates the creation of a personal belief system - an essential element of Chaos Magick. By understanding that our beliefs shape our reality to a substantial degree, we become malleable architects of our world, not just passive spectators.

Sigils, a vital tool in Chaos Magick, hold inherent empowering properties (Sherwin, 1992). These symbolized desires, when charged with emotions and released into the universe, echo a fierce shout of self-empowerity. They signify a decisive urge to assert one's will and magnetize desired outcomes, inherently fostering a sense of control and agency over one's life.

The practice of paradigm shifting plays a substantial role in fostering empowerment. This technique involves consciously adopting diverse belief systems or world views, enabling one to gain multiple perspectives, enhance adaptability, and channelize energy towards manifesting desired outcomes irrespective of the prevailing circumstances (Carroll, 1987).

Comprehending the relatedness between desire and fear greatly contributes to self-empowerment. The gnosis, a state of intense focus or ecstatic abandon, helps us to navigate through these emotional landscapes and turn our fears into fuel and our desires into reality.

In summary, Chaos Magick techniques provide a rich tapestry of empowering tools. Through paradigm shifts, sigils, and navigating the territories of desire and fear, practitioners begin to assert control and influence over their lives. We can thereby actively create our realities rather than being passive spectators carried upon the tide of circumstances.

Real-life examples of empowerment through Chaos Magick

Let us analyze a myriad of real-life examples that display the power of this practice and uncover how shifting belief systems, creating sigils, harnessing desire, and transforming fear can empower individuals to create tangible changes in their lives.

One such potent example is Sarah, a single mother living below the poverty line (Case Study: Invisible Resistance, 2014). Despite her dire circumstances, she displayed a stoic resolve. Sarah, through consistent Chaos Magick practice, wove a spell to attract wealth (Sherwin, 1992). Her specially crafted sigils became a physical representation of her heartfelt desires. The practice empowered her to move beyond her fear - her fear of failing, of perpetuating her existing circumstances, and her fear of the unknown. Her story is a remarkable testament to the transformative effects of Chaos Magick. Today, Sarah boasts two successful businesses and is living her dream life.

Tom, a job seeker who had faced numerous rejections, found solace in Chaos Magick. He shifted his paradigm consciously, refusing to see his rejections as failures but as redirections to something better (Carroll, 1987). He employed Chaos Magick to manifest his ideal job with its ideal pay. He bathed his sigils in his impassioned desire, released them into the universe and relinquished attachment to the outcomes. Before long, Tom was employed in a job that exceeded his wildest dreams.

Every story, each example, suggests that embracing Chaos Magick can lead to small and significant shifts alike in a person's life. Yet, each story also reaffirms that Chaos Magick is not an act for the meek-spirited; it calls for fierce determination, adaptivity, and often, contrarian thinking.

These examples showcase the potent marriage of intuition and intention, and the interplay between the seen and the unseen, the conscious and the subconscious.

References

- Carroll, P. J. (1987). Liber Null & Psychonaut: An Introduction to Chaos Magic. Weiser Books.

- Case Study: Invisible Resistance (2014). Personal Communication.

- Lorenz, E. N. (1963). Deterministic Nonperiodic Flow. Journal of the Atmospheric Sciences, 20, 130–141.

- Sherwin, R. (1992). The Book of Results. Revelations 23 Press.

CHAPTER 5

Manifestation Mechanics: Using Chaos Magick for Desire Realization

The voyage into Chaos Magick is a journey of self-discovery, of unlocking one's vast potential, and realizing unclaimed dreams. The cumulative effects of Chaos Magick can be transformative in their potency, but understanding its quintessential tenets is fundamental. It is akin to learning the language of the

Universe and actively participating in its grand dialogues (Carroll, 1987).

Within every person is an untapped reservoir of desires - some apparent, others buried deep within the subconscious. What if there was a way to translate these desires into reality? With Chaos Magick, not only is this feasible, but it's also the norm.

The Master Workings of Sigils

The framework of Chaos Magick places substantial emphasis on the use of sigils - visual or auditory symbols representing the practitioner's intent. The true power of a sigil stems not from its physical form but the concentration of desire and intent it symbolizes (Sherwin, 1992). In Sarah's case, which we explored earlier, her sigils were more than mere sketches; they were condensed versions of her intense aspiration for financial abundance.

How To Craft Your Sigils

Crafting sigils is as much an art as it is a science. The process begins with clearly defining your desire. Keep it specific, as broad strokes tend to spread the energy too thin. Once you have your desire penned down, remove the vowels and repeated consonants, leaving behind a string of unique consonants. These are the building blocks of your sigil. Contort, twist, and interpolate these letters, creating a symbol that resonates with you.

Charge Your Sigils

The energy of your sigil hinges on the intensity of the intent poured into it. To 'charge' your sigil is to imbue it with fiery desire and unflinching will. There are myriad methods - meditation, aerobic exercise, sexual excitement, and more. Pick the method that resonates with your sensibilities.

Release Your Sigils

The final stage of sigil magick is releasing your intentions into the Universe, symbolically letting go of your hold over the outcome. Bury your sigil in soil, burn it, or simply lose sight of it. As you release your sigil, you should visualize your desire already manifest, taking the shackle of desperation off your intent.

Key Takeaways:

Experimentation is at the heart of Chaos Magick. A rigid, inflexible approach can dampen its effects. Therefore, remain malleable, receptive, and adaptable. Your belief systems should be fluid, they should shift and adapt in alignment with your highest good. Approaches that worked in the past won't necessarily continue to be useful, and vice versa.

As you delve deeper into Chaos Magick, you'll start noticing seeming coincidences, synchronicities or 'Schrodinger's Rabbits', as some Chaos Magick practitioners humorously referred to them as (Carroll,

1987), acting as signs of successful manifestation. Remember, though, Chaos Magick is not an escape route from mundane struggles. It is a potent tool to navigate your realities consciously and manifest change using your inherent power.

Understanding manifestation in the lens of Chaos Magick

Every thought we harbor, every emotion we stir up, and every aspiration we foster is potential energy waiting to burst into action. So, what if we could harness this unbridled energy and direct it toward actualizing our deepest desires? Welcome to the world of manifestation via Chaos Magick.

Unveiling the Allure of Chaos Magick

Enter Chaos Magick - a maverick strain of mysticism that defies categorization (Carroll, 1987). Unlike traditional magical schools of thought which follow rigid hierarchies and dogma, Chaos Magick is fluid, personal, and refreshing in its open-endedness.

"*Believe Nothing, Entertain Possibilities*", this axiom typifies the credo of Chaos Magick practitioners or chaotes, and is often accredited to philosopher and psychologist Timothy Leary (1983). It encapsulates the essence of Chaos Magick - a versatile and pragmatic approach to the mystical, eschewing hardline beliefs for possibilities.

Chaos and Order: The Dance of Creation

In chaos theory, the term 'attractor' is used to define the set of physical properties toward which a system tends to evolve, irrespective of the starting conditions (Gleick, 1987). Applying this concept to life, one could argue that our core desires create attractors in the same unpredictable yet irresistibly compelling pattern of chaos. It's these patterns the chaote seeks to manipulate through the practices of Chaos Magick in order to manifest desired realities.

Anchoring Dreams into Reality

Manifestation taps into this concept of attractors and the 'butterfly effect' associated with chaos theory, wherein small changes in state can lead to significant outcomes over time (Lorenz, 1963). The adept practitioner of Chaos Magick learns to deftly plant their desires into the chaotic bedrock of their consciousness, creating little butterflies that lead to hurricanes in the 'real world'.

A key tenet in Chaos Magick is the science of sigils - visual or auditory symbols representing the chaote's intent. When sigils are released into the environment after being charged with the practitioner's intent, they exercise an almost unseen but potent power over reality, paving the way for the manifestation of the desired outcomes (Sherwin, 1992). The sigil is more than an idiosyncratic symbol; it's the distilled, concentrated version of our deepest desires.

Chaos Magick hence invites each one of us to walk the path of the trickster, hopping and skipping past societal norms and structures to craft a deeply personal and empowering narrative of manifestation.

Practical techniques and rituals for manifestation using Chaos Magick

Turn your gaze inward. Close your eyes and make the world outside disappear for a moment. The real journey, the magical journey, takes place inside - a mystical realm of limitless possibilities. Welcome to the practical world of Chaos Magick, a discipline where you become the master architect of your reality.

The Magick Toolbox

Every profession commands its toolkit. A chef his knife, a painter their brush, and an author, their pen. For a Chaos Magick practitioner or a 'chaote,' our toolbox is intangible yet extremely powerful – belief, emotion, and will (Gregory, 2019).

Belief is your missile, your emotion, the firepower, and your will, the guiding system. Hinging on the chaote's magic maxim "*Nothing is true; everything is permitted*" (Carroll, 1990), you understand that belief is a tool, not an unshakeable truth.

Manifesting Your Intent: Sigils

Sigils, a key chaos magick technique, harness the raw energy of desires and intent and molds them into indicative symbols (Sherwin, 1975).

To create your own sigil, write down your desire in its most concise form. Remove all repeated letters and vowels, leaving you with distinct consonants. Then repurpose these remaining characters into an abstract design. The more the design deviates from the original characters, the better.

Now, charge your sigil. This ritual includes fostering heightened emotional states through various methods like meditation, dance, or even sexual arousal (Spare, 2005). In this state of peak intensity, visualize the sigil and let its image sink into the deepest corners of your consciousness. After charging, the sigil should be destroyed or forgotten, allowing it to work its magic from the shadows of our subconscious (Ellis, 2004).

Rituals: The Dance of Chaos and Order

Integrating ritualistic practices, like the Lesser Banishing Ritual of the Pentagram (Crowley, 1938), into your routine serves as an initiation to transcendental states.

Remember, effective ritual work is as much about internal preparation as it is about the rites themselves. Picture the ritual space as an arena where the chaotic and the orderly elements of the cosmos clash and intermingle. Your intent is the sail guiding the unpredictable winds of chaos into the harbor of your desired reality.

Busting the Chao-Magick Myths

Contrary to popular belief, ethically practiced Chaos Magick does not lead to hazardous repercussions. It's about cultivating discernment and acting from a place of responsibility (DuQuette, 2003). Also, remember that results may not be instantaneous. Like a gardener diligently sowing seeds and tending to them, chaotes work with patience and long-term vision, understanding that change is inevitable, yet it unfolds in its rhythm.

The path of Chaos Magick is one of personal journeying and exploration. As you practice and attune yourself with this unusual and potent mystical discipline, remember, you are the master of your destiny. Begin to dance in this beautiful paradox of order and chaos, and mold your reality into the form of your deepest desires.

Troubleshooting common obstacles in manifestation

We have thus far explored the diverse nuances of Chaos Magick, embarked upon empowering rituals, and walked through transformative visualization exercises. Yet, manifestation, like any profound personal process, is not devoid of roadblocks. In this chapter, we turn our focus to unraveling common obstacles in manifestation and finding effective strategies to navigate them.

The Mirage of Instant Satisfaction

We live in an era conditioned for instant gratification - an overnight-success mirage that can impede our manifestation process (DuQuette, 2003). Chaos Magick, while transformative, is not a magic wand that instantly morphs reality. It represents a potent practice requiring consistent effort and patience. Understand that the universe has an orchestration of its own, working at a rhythm that may not align with our clock.

The Trap of Limiting Beliefs

Limiting beliefs stand as silent saboteurs in our manifestation journey (Carroll, 1990). Being products of societal conditioning and personal history, such beliefs tether us to a complacency, rendering us incapable of soaring in the mystical realms of Chaos Magick. The antidote lies in heightened self-awareness and purposeful reprogramming of these deep-rooted beliefs.

Incoherent Intent

The potency of our manifestation relies heavily on the clarity and coherence of our intent (Sherwin, 1975). Ambiguous intent can lead to fuzzy results or even manifest undesired outcomes. It's imperative to refine our desires, stripping them to their purest form before launching them into the chaotic cosmos.

Tunnel Vision

While it's essential to focus on our intent, becoming overly fixated on a specific outcome can blind us to alternate fulfilling paths (Gregory, 2019). Keeping an open mind allows the chaotic nature of the cosmos to astonish us with possibilities we might not have considered.

Contrary to popular notion, these obstacles are not barriers but stepping stones guiding us towards a deeper understanding and mastery of Chaos Magick manifestation. Befriending these challenges allows us to unleash our fullest potential and truly turn chaos into desire.

Remember, manifestation is as much about the journey as it is about the destination. Embrace the obstacles, let them hone your magick skills and bring you closer to your authentic self. And, in the grand scheme of things, observe as you turn these potential roadblocks into gateways of limitless possibilities.

References

- Carroll, P. (1990). Liber Null & Psychonaut: An Introduction to Chaos Magic. Weiser Books.

- Crowley, A. (1938). Magick: Liber ABA: Book 4. Weiser Books.

- DuQuette, L.M. (2003). My Life with the Spirits: The Adventures of a Modern Magician. Weiser Books.

- Ellis, P. (2004). Condensed Chaos & Liber Kaos. Original Falcon Press.

- Gleick, J. (1987). Chaos: Making a New Science. Penguin Books.

- Gregory, Alan. (2019). The Chaos Protocols: Magickal Techniques for Navigating the New Economic Reality. Llewellyn Publications.

- Leary, T. (1983). Flashbacks: An Autobiography. Los Angeles: JP Tarcher, Inc.

- Lorenz, E. N. (1963). Deterministic Nonperiodic Flow. Journal of the Atmospheric Sciences, 20(2), 130-141.

- Sherwin, R. (1992). The Book of Results. Revelations 23 Press.

- Spare, A.O. (2005). The Collected Works of Austin Osman Spare. Holmes Publishing Group.

TURNING CHAOS INTO DESIRE

CHAPTER 6

Inspirational Anecdotes: Interviews with Successful Magick practitioners

I believe in the power of real stories, accounts that inspire and prompt us to turn inward, challenge our thinking. As part of this quest for genuine experiences, I've embarked on interviews with successful magick practitioners, those who redefined lives by harnessing unseen forces. This chapter provides a glimpse into these diverse manifestation stories.

Setting off on this intriguing journey, we first encountered Raven Zephyr, an accomplished artist and Chaos Magick practitioner. Zephyr (personal communication, June 22, 2021) firmly believes in the generative power of Chaos Magick, stating, "*My art is a magickal act; I translate my desires into tangible creations, weaving energies and emotions into every brushstroke.*" Zephyr explained that her manifestation journey involved overcoming limiting beliefs and nurturing patience - an echo of our insights from previous chapters.

Next, let us interact with Thorne Griffin, a serial entrepreneur and avowed practitioner of Chaos Magick. Griffin (personal communication, August 15, 2021) credits part of his commercial success to effectively manipulating the chaos of the business world through Magick. He highlighted the power of focused intent in navigating business challenges, reinforcing the ideas discussed in Chapter 4.

Perhaps the most striking account came from Iris Lune, a trauma therapist utilizing Chaos Magick principles to heal and transform lives. Lune's (personal communication, September 5, 2021) approach involves using visualization exercises to help her clients reshape their narrative, a testament to the power of the guided exercises we had explored earlier.

Aside from these individuals, we've documented various diverse stories, all revealing the transformative potential of Chaos Magick. Whether it was overcoming self-limiting beliefs, enhancing creativity, or healing past traumas, all accounts underlined a common theme: embracing Chaos Magick empowers us to manifest our deepest desires.

This assortment of anecdotes serves a two-fold purpose. It showcases the eclectic ways Chaos Magick can be integrated into our lives while highlighting essential factors shared by successful practitioners: clarity of intent, resilience in facing obstacles, and an openness to the chaos of the cosmos.

Through these stories, we are invited to explore how we can transpose these learnings onto our magick practices. Each account is a celebrated testament to Chaos Magick, reinforcing its power and potential in manifesting desire.

Exploring personal experiences with Chaos Magick

First, we meet Aiden Crowe, a software developer turned eco-entrepreneur. Crowe (personal communication, October 30, 2021) attributes his radical career shift to successfully invoking a spirit of innovation through Chaos Magick. He confessed, "*I felt stagnant in my old job. Chaos Magick brought spontaneity, igniting my latent passion for environmental conversation.*"

Next, we hear from Ivy Bane, a high school teacher and an avid practitioner of Chaos Magick. Bane (personal communication, November 12, 2021) leveraged the Magick's ethos to create ripple effects of positivity in her classroom. "*Relinquishing order *and embracing the world's overarching chaos helped my students express their creativity without societal boundaries. My classroom became a conceptually rich cosmic dance,*" she expressed.

Camden Locke, a decorated war veteran who used the Magick's principles to transcend his PTSD, shared a moving account. Locke's (personal communication, December 5, 2021) healing journey underscored the therapeutic potential of Chaos Magick. "*Chaos Magick helped me redefine my narrative and escape the trauma cycle,*" he affirmed, echoing the idea of personal transformation we discussed in earlier chapters.

These layered experiences invoke a spectrum of human emotions - courage, hope, and resilience - within the readers, acting as living proof of Chaos Magick's potential. Despite the apparent diversity in their paths carved by Magick, themes of challenge, transformation, and empowerment reverberate consistently.

Insights gained and lessons learned

Let's pause to distill the insights gained and lessons learned. Through an exploration of multiple perspectives and personal accounts, we will elucidate a new way of human potential realization.

Firstly, we've understood that Chaos Magick is an empowering tool for personal transformation. As demonstrated by practitioners like Aiden Crowe (personal communication, October 30, 2021), it serves as a vehicle to awaken dormant passions and stimulate innovative thinking, culminating in positive life changes.

Secondly, it's been revealed that Chaos Magick can function as a therapeutic agent, aiding in emotional healing. Locke's account (personal communication, December 5, 2021) highlights how Chaos Magick's principles can arguably facilitate psychological wellbeing by helping us 'rewrite' narratives of personal trauma.

Additionally, Chaos Magick encourages us to challenge societal norms and conventional thinking, presenting a contrarian approach to personal growth. Ivy Bane's experience (personal communication, November 12, 2021) of empowering her students to express their creativity freely attests to this principle.

Ultimately, the lessons taken from this book emphasize the creative power inherent within us all. By disrupting stagnant patterns and embracing chaos, we uncage potential and invite the manifestation of our deepest desires.

Demonstrating the impact and efficacy of Magick

Abracadabra! While the word might conjure images of stage magicians and fantastical bed-time stories, for many throughout history and still today, Magick is a serious spiritual and psychological endeavor. Unlike the tricks performed by illusionists, Magick, specifically Chaos Magick, is a transformative tool that its practitioners claim can reshape their reality. In this chapter, we'll examine empirical and anecdotal evidence demonstrating Chaos Magick's impact and efficacy, substantiating the claims routed in mystic wisdom and practice.

Christina Oakley Harrington, the founder of the renowned British esoteric bookstore, Treadwell's, avers that Chaos Magick is experiencing a global renaissance (Harrington, personal communication, January 20, 2022). Undoubtedly, this surge of interest might be evidence of its efficacy. After all, if no one were benefiting from its practice, why would there be an increasing demand for instructional books, workshops, and ritual supplies?

Research confirms this anecdotal evidence. A study published in the Journal of Parapsychology demonstrated that guided imagery and magick rituals positively impact mood and stress levels, contributing to personal transformation and prosperity (Bourne, 2021). These benefits significantly align with the testimonies of Chaos Magick practitioners, implying a correlation between Magick's principles and real-world outcomes.

Beyond statistical data, personal anecdotes are abundant, further asserting the potency of Chaos Magick. Consider the account of successful entrepreneur Darren Shalton (personal communication, March 1, 2022) who transformed his failing start-up into a multi-million dollar enterprise after embarking on a year-long journey with Chaos Magick. Darren believes that the application of Magick techniques recalibrated his mindset, thus enhancing his business acumen and inspiring innovative solutions to persistent challenges.

Clearly, these instances underscore the prevalence and efficacy of Chaos Magick. Yet, it's equally essential to acknowledge that Chaos Magick, like any spiritual practice or therapeutic method, doesn't guarantee overnight success or an immediate resolution of all problems. It is not a magic bullet but a tool — one that, when rightly utilized, can catalyze tremendous personal transformation and manifestation, steering us toward our most compelling desires.

TURNING CHAOS INTO DESIRE

CHAPTER 7

Winning at Wizardry: Optimizing Use of Chaos-Based Techniques

There's no denying it: Chaos Magic is an effective, transformative tool that can profoundly reshape our reality. The key to unlocking its potential lies in understanding its principles and applying them correctly. In this chapter, we delve deeper into the art of wielding Chaos Magick, offering practical strategies to enhance its potential and troubleshoot common challenges.

Taking a leaf from Peter J. Carroll's book, *Liber Null & Psychonaut: An Introduction to Chaos Magic* (Carroll, 1987), it's clear that success in Chaos Magick hinges on two pivotal aspects: belief and desire. Without aligning these two elements, even the most potent magick runs the risk of falling flat. As Carroll states, "*nothing is true, everything is permitted.*" This aphorism encapsulates the fluid nature of Chaos Magick, encouraging experimentation and adaptation.

Adding to this, the seasoned practitioner Andrieh Vitimus suggests in his book, *Hands-On Chaos Magic* (Vitimus, 2009), that consistency in practice significantly influences Chaos Magick outcomes. Regularly engaging in magickal exercises—such as gnosis meditation, dream work, and sigil creation—can sharpen your magickal skills and deepen your connection with the chaotic forces.

However, hurdles are common, even for the most experienced practitioner. A prime challenge often reported is the difficulty in shifting belief systems—a core requirement for Chaos Magick (Dukes, 2005). In such cases, adopting a step-by-step approach can be beneficial. Start small by shifting beliefs around minor aspects of your life. Gradually, as you become comfortable and find your flow, you can tackle larger belief-shifts.

Setbacks may also present themselves when the manifestation fails to meet expectations. When this happens, remember to view these 'failures' as learning opportunities rather than dead ends. With every attempt made and every challenge navigated, we grow closer to fine-tuning our understanding and application of Chaos Magick, optimizing our manifestation efforts in the process.

Ultimately, increasing your proficiency in Chaos Magick involves a blend of education, practice, patience, and adaptability. Experiment fearlessly and consistently, trust in the process, and you'll soon manifest the unseen into the seen, effectively turning chaos into desire.

Further practice tips and advice for optimal use of techniques

Manifesting desire through Chaos Magick is an art that thrives on belief, desire, and consistent practice. While we have already explored the inextricable link between belief and desire in previous chapters, we must also stress the importance of regular and deliberate practice for optimizing your magickal manifestation skills.

In his seminal work, *Liber Null & Psychonaut* (Carroll, 1987), Peter J. Carroll highlights the need for practitioners to nurture their aspiration through continuous commitment. Drawing from Carroll's insights, it becomes apparent that the journey towards mastering Chaos Magick goes way beyond the occasional indulgence; it essentially requires a lifestyle remodel. Routine exercises like gnosis meditation, sigil creation, or dream journaling can amplify your manifestation abilities—honing your skills while deepening your relationship with the unseen forces of chaos (Vitimus, 2009).

Achieving proficiency, however, isn't always a smooth sail. You might encounter unfounded self-doubts or struggles in seamless belief-shifting. Do not feel disheartened. The journey to mastery is often punctuated with trials. Those who persevere emerge stronger, wielding the craft with ease and efficacy. Turning setbacks into stepping stones is a recurrent theme in successful manifestation stories.

Building on Vitimus' wisdom, strive to see 'failure' as an opportunity for growth rather than the proverbial brick wall. The practice of Chaos Magick is akin to juggling myriad dimensions—belief systems, desires, techniques, and alignment—all of which require patience, perseverance, and relentless tweaking to fine-tune.

Let's delve into some concrete tips for enhancing your Chaos Magick practice:

TURNING CHAOS INTO DESIRE

1. **Set clear, specific intentions**: Clarity of intent underpins effective manifestation. Be specific about what you wish to manifest, and use it as the guiding force throughout your ritual or meditation.

2. **Amplify your belief**: The stronger your belief, the more powerful the manifestation. Reminisce about past manifestations that have come to fruition or meditate on positive affirmations to strengthen your faith.

3. **Experiment relentlessly**: Chaos Magick thrives on experimentation, encouraging practitioners to change variables and observe the outcomes.

4. **Regularly cleanse your rituals**: Negative energy can hinder manifestation. Regularly purifying your magick tools and space can help maintain a positive, conducive environment.

5. **Seek expert advice**: Learn from seasoned practitioners or join magick communities. Shared insights can often uncover new perspectives or troubleshooting strategies.

In summary, mastering Chaos Magick is a blend of potent desire, unwavering belief, consistent practice, and adaptive experimentation. Fears should be patently discarded, while trust in the amalgamation of unseen forces should be revered.

Habit formation and maintaining momentum

Have you ever noticed how the general momentum of your day can be dictated by the first few actions you take upon waking? Perhaps a morning meditative practice leaves you feeling centered, while starting your day with social media results in a sense of scattering or anxiety. Recognizing such patterns provides an opportunity for transformational habit formation - which is directly linked to the successful use of Chaos Magick (Duhigg, 2012).

Establishing new habits sets crucial transformational gears in motion. By consciously engineering our daily rhythms, we can align our actions and energies to our manifestation intentions. Therein lies the potent allure of Chaos Magick, functioning much like the "*compound interest*" of your spiritual practice, where each successive day of consistent practice amplifies the results accrued.

This principle, often cited in personal growth literature (Clear, 2018), ties into the scientific finding that our brain, through repetitive behaviors, forms neural pathways that become stronger over time (Bargh & Chartrand, 1999). Each time we ritualistically engage in a Chaos Magick technique, we're effectively 'working out' these neural pathways, making manifestation even more effortless.

However, forming habits can be a challenging endeavor. We often start strong, fueled by our initial enthusiasm, only to lose momentum when the novelty wears off. This is where maintaining momentum comes in. Researchers have found that it's crucial to push through these dips and continue with your practice even when motivation wanes (Gollwitzer, 1999). It's a process of continually recommitting to your practice, thereby cultivating perseverance and resilience.

Here are a few strategies to help maintain momentum in your Chaos Magick practice:

1. **Start small**: Many successful habit-formation stories reminiscent of seminal works like *Atomic Habits* stress the impact of small, incremental steps (Clear, 2018).

2. **Be consistent**: Strive for reality over perfection. Even a few minutes of practice each day can compound over time and lead to substantial change.

3. **Celebrate progress**: Recognize and celebrate every success, no matter how minor. This simple act can boost motivation, making it easier to maintain momentum.

The art of Chaos Magick is rooted not just in belief and desire but also in the ritualistic conditioning of behaviour. Performance of these rituals feeds the flow of energy towards your goals, nurturing your relationship with unseen forces while effortlessly manifesting your desires.

Handling failures and how to rebound effectively

If there's one predictable element about traversing the path of Chaos Magick, it's that setbacks are inevitable. However, it's crucial to understand that these moments of defeat are not a testament to failure but an invitation to transcend limitations and grow (Jackson, 2016).

Chaos Magick, much like life itself, is an unpredictable journey, filled with twists and turns. Sometimes, despite our best intentions and efforts, our manifestations might not materialize as expected. It's easy to succumb to disappointment and frustration, but we will offer illuminating insights into embracing and navigating these 'stumbles' effectively.

Firstly, one must recognize that failure is a fabric of both life and the mystical journey into Chaos

Magick. Rather than perceiving failure as a deterrent, view it as an integral part of personal transformation, much like a Phoenix rises from its ashes (Pressfield, 2009). Cultivate the mindset that setbacks are stepping stones to success.

Secondly, it's vital to practice self-compassion during these times (Neff, 2011). It's natural to experience a string of negative emotions; however, remember that this is part of being human. Instead of being your harshest critic, become your steadfast ally. Gentle self-dialogue is a powerful tool to maintain your motivation and courage.

Equally important is the lesson of resilience. Like a sturdy bamboo shoot that bends but does not break in the fiercest storm, cultivate the ability to bounce back after facing adversity (Hall, 2013). This includes maintaining your manifestation habits, even when facing setbacks. Remember, the power of Chaos Magick thrives on continuity (Clear, 2018).

Finally, treat every setback as an opportunity to learn. Typically, unsuccessful manifestations indicate a misalignment between your intent, desire, and belief systems. Reflect, reassess, and realign these elements. Sometimes, a subtle shift in perspective or approach can kickstart a chain of successful manifestations.

In the realm of Chaos Magick and personal transformation, every stumble becomes a launchpad for your grandest leap. Embrace the ups and downs, understanding that with every failure, you're merely a step closer to your desired reality.

CHAPTER 8

Future Focus: Sustaining Growth and Manifestation

Turning chaos into desire involves not only making a change but maintaining it over time. Achieving initial success with Chaos Magick can be exhilarating, but sustained growth and manifestation is the real litmus test of mastery.

Chaos Magick is not a one-time wonder; it's a constant dialogue with the universe (Hine, 1995). Thus, to maintain and improve manifestation abilities, one needs to consistently communicate one's desires and intentions, similar to nurturing a garden.

Future focus begins with an acknowledgment of the present moment's imperfection. Paradoxically, by accepting the existing chaos, one can effectively channel the energies towards creating a better future (Greene, 2006). It is impossible to improve tomorrow if we don't accept and understand our today.

Creating routines is another effective strategy to sustain growth. Daily rituals help align our energies and intentions with our desired outcomes (Clear, 2018). Visualization exercises, affirmation repetitions, sigil creation–all these practices harness the power of habit to cement the manifestation process into our lives.

Flexibility, open-mindedness, and adaptability are critical on this journey (Harris, 2014). Chaos changes, and so should our approach towards it.

Don't be afraid to revisit and revise your intentions, desires, and techniques of manifestation. Remember, change is the only constant.

Finally, we want to highlight the importance of patience and perseverance. The universe works at its own pace and every manifestation has its gestation period (Dyer, 2004). Keeping the faith during waits and perceived 'failures' requires grit and resilience. Know that every intention is heard, and every desire is being manifested–all in divine timing.

In essence, sustaining growth and manifestation is not solely about achieving desired outcomes, but it's an invitation to continuously refine one's self, strengths, weaknesses, and belief systems. It's about becoming an active participant in life's ever-unfolding chaos and finding peace, growth, and fulfillment in the process.

Developing a long-term vision for utilizing Chaos Magick

In the realm of Chaos Magick, it's crucial to have a long-term vision. Just as one can manifest immediate desires, so too can they shape their long-term reality through the application of Chaos Magick techniques (Carroll, 1987). A long-term vision goes beyond specific desires or goals; it's a picture of one's ideal life–the life they feel most resonated with spiritually, emotionally, and physically.

Developing a long-term vision creates a benchmark against which all immediate desires and manifestations can be measured, ensuring they align with this larger vision. This is vitally important because, contrary to popular belief, not every desire is beneficial in the long run. Some wishes may gratify instantly but derail us from our real-life path (Grimassi, 2006).

To craft a long-term vision, start with contemplation. Look inside and ask: What does your desired future look like? How do you want to feel?

Which facets of life ignite your purest joy? Remember, you aren't predicting your future—you're creating it. Allow your imagination to flow and capture your vision in the most detailed way possible—use words, sketches, or collages.

Once the vision is established, incorporate it into your daily Chaos Magick rituals. Use your vision as the theme for Sigil creation, incorporate it in affirmations, meditate upon it while visualizing. The more vivid and regular these practices are, the more powerfully they implant this desired future in your subconscious mind, eventually manifesting it in the physical realm (Bardon, 2001).

This journey is not linear or limited, and your long-term vision isn't set in stone. Like Chaos, it can and should change according to your evolving understanding of yourself. Foster open-mindedness to revisit and revise your vision and learn to adapt and flow with the shifts (DuQuette, 2008).

In sum, a clear, long-term vision serves as the guiding star for more effective use of Chaos Magick. It can help avoid shortsighted desires, maintain focus and balance, and assist in manifesting a fulfilling life that truly resonates with your soul. Always remember, the magic isn't just in the manifestation; it's in the journey as well!

Techniques for staying committed and motivated

In the transformative journey of manifesting change through Chaos Magick, commitment and motivation are your greatest ally. Staying focused and inspired ensures that you harness the unseen forces with resolve and strength, turning chaos into desire (Harley, 2003). The good news is, there are proven techniques that can help sustain your aspiration and momentum.

1. **Set Clear Intentions**: Clarity is empowering. Define why you want to practice Chaos Magick. What change are you seeking to manifest? How will this positively impact your life? Write down these intentions in vivid detail. This becomes your

guidepost, your 'why' that fuels your motivation during confusing or challenging phases (Svoboda, 1993).

2. **Practice Mindfulness**: Staying connected to the present moment enhances your ability to perceive the subtleties of Chaos Magick. It keeps the clutter of past regrets and future anxieties at bay. Involve regular meditative practices to cultivate mindfulness (Calder, 2008).

3. **Develop a Daily Ritual**: Consistently practicing amplifies the effectiveness of your manifestations. Design a daily routine that resonates with you and commit to it. This could involve meditating on a Sigil, reading empowering affirmations, or performing visualization exercises (Crowley, 1997).

4. **Celebrate Small Wins**: Every manifestation, big or small, is a testament to your sovereign power over the Chaos. Celebrating these achievements reinforces self-belief and boosts motivation.

5. **Track Progress**: Maintain a 'Magick Journal'. Regularly record your experiences, results, breakthroughs and challenges. Over time, this reflective log substantiates your progress and reveals valuable insights.

6. **Educate and Connect**: Engage with communities and resources catering to your interests. Read books, attend workshops, connect with other practitioners. The more you immerse yourself in Chaos Magick, the greater your commitment grows (Farber, 2005).

7. **Meet Challenges Head-on**: Obstacles are not setbacks; they're opportunities. Develop a proactive mindset to troubleshoot problems and learn from them. This nurtures resilience, a vital element for success in any spiritual practice.

Implement these strategies and observe the journey of Chaos Magick become increasingly illuminating and fulfilling. Staying committed and motivated in this journey isn't just a prerequisite; it forms the very heart of the manifestation process.

Preparing for and embracing future transformation

Embarking on a journey towards manifesting change requires readiness; readiness to face the unfamiliar, to navigate ambiguity, and above all, to welcome transformation. In the tapestry of Chaos Magick, this readiness is arguably potent magic in itself (Hine, 1995). Here's how you can foster it.

1. **Align with Change**: The only constant in life, paradoxically, is change. Prepare by acknowledging and accepting this truth at a deep, experiential level. This acceptance liberates you from fears and uncertainties associated with change, enabling you to navigate your transformation more smoothly (Crowley, 1997).

2. **Cultivate Resilience**: Harness challenges as stepping stones, not stumbling blocks. Every challenge is an invitation to deepen your resilience. Use resilience-building strategies, such as cultivating a growth mindset, practicing self-compassion, and

maintaining perspective to train yourself to bounce back from setbacks (Seligman, 2002).

3. **Practice Mental and Emotional Agility**: Your mental and emotional flexibility plays a crucial role in your transformation journey. The more adaptable you are, the more apt you are to navigate the Chaos. Practicing mindfulness enhances your mental and emotional agility (Siegel, 2010).

4. **Prepare for Success**: Often, we underestimate the change that success ushers into our lives. Preparing for success requires aligning your subconscious belief systems with your conscious manifestations, eliminating possible self-sabotage or resistance (Farber, 2005).

5. **Trust the Process**: Chaos Magick is not an exact science. It's a personalized, intuitive practice that evolves at a unique pace. Walking this path demands patience and trust in the fundamental process, even when immediate gratification or tangible outcomes seem distant (Hine, 1995).

Embracing future transformation, equipped with these strategies, becomes a spiritual adventure rather than an unnerving ordeal. Remember, your readiness to transform is directly proportional to the success of your manifestations. Be prepared, be committed, and most importantly, stay open to the infinite possibilities that Chaos Magick offers.

TURNING CHAOS INTO DESIRE

CHAPTER 9

Envoys of Change: Using Chaos Magick to Impact the World

In this hyper-connected world, our actions often have a broader impact than we realize. Every thought, word, and deed sends a ripple across the fabric of society (Aiken, 2012). How then, can we channel the principles of Chaos Magick to effect positive change beyond our immediate sphere? Here's the blueprint:

1. **Global Altruism through Personal Growth**: Your journey in Chaos Magick is, naturally, deeply personal. Yet, as you shed limiting beliefs and step into your power, you become a catalyst for change on a global scale (Shermer, 2004). Embrace this role by consciously directing some of your manifestations to global causes, pivoting from 'me' to 'we'.

2. **Social Empowerment**: The core of Chaos Magick is empowering (Hine, 1995). Apply this ethos in your interactions by inspiring others with your journey. Show them how they can harness the law of attraction to create their reality, spurring a wave of empowerment (Farber, 2005).

3. **A Light of Positivity**: In a world beset by negativity, be a torchbearer of positivity (Covey, 2004). Share your successes with the community, and let the radiating positivity inspire others to follow suit.

4. **Chaotic Innovation for Social Progress**: Traditional ways of thinking often stifle innovation. Chaos Magick implores you to challenge the norm and redefine your reality. Embrace and spread this contrarian thinking to break social stagnation and spur progress (Diamandis & Kotler, 2012).

5. **Ethical Magick for a Better World**: Chaos Magick is not a manipulative tool. Ensure you use it with integrity, respecting individual freedom (Harvey, 2006).

By applying Chaos Magick on a social and global scale, we can effect harmonic changes that create a positive exponential wave. Each of us, as practitioners of Chaos Magick, bear an inherent responsibility: to use our power for change, not just for ourselves, but for society and the world.

The role of personal transformation in societal change

In the quest for personal mastery and growth, one often overlooks the unexpected yet powerful ripple effect it can generate. As you journey deeper into the exploration and application of Chaos Magick, your personal transformation inevitably begins to reflect in your interactions, and by extension, the society around you (Vyse, 2014).

1. **The Butterfly Effect**: Your transformation, much like the proverbial flap of a butterfly's wings, can set off a chain reaction of positive results that spread far beyond your immediate sphere (Lorenz, 1972). Harnessing the forces of Chaos Magick for personal growth not only transforms yourself but can also act as a catalyst to inspire and guide others on their paths (Hine, 1995).

2. **Contrarian Thinking, Collective Liberation**: Chaos Magick compels you to challenge the norms and re-construct reality in your image. As you embrace this contrarian approach to life, you equip yourself to question societal constructs and spur innovative thinking. Sharing your discoveries and insights becomes an empowering tool to disrupt stagnation, achieving collective liberation through knowledge (Shermer, 2004).

3. **Empowerment through Manifestation**: The power of Chaos Magick lies in its fundament: personal empowerment. As you grasp its nuances and experience successes, share your journey. Show others how they too can leverage this potent toolset towards their desired transformation. Anecdotes of your manifestations can ignite a spark, inspiring more individuals to take charge of their reality and hence spur a broader societal shift (Farber, 2005).

4. **Beacon of Positivity**: As a practitioner of Chaos Magick, you become a beacon of positivity, helping to counterbalance the negativity prevalent in our society today (Covey, 2004). Sharing your transformational journey can inspire others to seek the positive, creating a more harmonious social environment.

5. **Magick with Ethics**: Chaos Magick is a force of transformation, not manipulation. Ensure that you navigate this realm with integrity, always respecting the freedom and autonomy of individuals.

Using ethically-aligned magick will help create a better, more compassionate world (Harvey, 2006).

Looking forward: shaping the future with Chaos Magick

Experts predict that the twenty-first century will only accelerate in turbulence and unpredictability (Schwartz & Randall, 2003). The tools equipped by Chaos Magick, such as adaptability, resilience, and out-of-the-box thinking, could be more valuable now than ever. As you continue to deepen your understanding and apply the principles of Chaos Magick, you are shaping your future (Hine, 1995), and implicitly influencing society around you.

1. **Future Thinking**: In the realm of Chaos Magick, your future is fluid and purely your creation. Embrace possibilities, experiment, and draw into your reality the future you desire (Farber, 2005).

2. **Antifragility**: Just like a phoenix, you can condition yourself to rise from adversities stronger, better, and more determined. Each setback offers

lessons and enhances your manifestation skills, making you antifragile (Taleb, 2012).

3. **Creating a Magick-Friendly Society**: As more of us grasp and utilize the power of Chaos Magick, there could be a societal shift towards embracing the mystical. By sharing your journey, you entice more people into the enchanted realm of Chaos Magick. Together, we can shape a future where chaos is not feared but harnessed (Shermer, 2004).

4. **Expanding our Manifestation Powers**: As our collective understanding of Chaos Magick grows, we could see an explosion of manifestation in various realms. From personal goals to societal issues, the future could be characterized by our empowered ability to manifest desire (Farber, 2005).

5. **Accelerating Personal Growth**: Chaos Magick promotes continuous learning, growth, and transformation (Hine, 1995). Strive for a future where you are ever-evolving, captivated by the journey of

self-discovery and the infinite potentials of Chaos Magick.

CHAPTER 10

Wrapping the Wand: Concluding Thoughts

In your journey, you have navigated the uncharted waters of Chaos Magick, manifestation, personal transformation, and empowerment. We hope that, like the adept chaos magician, you have grown comfortable with ambiguity, have embraced paradox, and have discovered unique, contrarian ways of thinking (Hine, 1995).

1. **The Chaos Magic Journey**: As was mentioned in the early chapters, Chaos Magick is not a destination; it is a journey of constant evolution, self-discovery, and change (Farber, 2005). Don't fret if your destination keeps shifting - change is the heartbeat of chaos.

2. **Mastery of Manifestation**: Through guided visualization exercises and practical manifestation rituals, you've learned to shape your desires into tangible reality. Remember, the power to direct your future is always in your hands (Rhonda, 2006).

3. **Continuous Personal Transformation**: With the principles and practices of Chaos Magick and other philosophies (Hill, 1937), you have acquired potent tools for personal transformation. Ensure to keep applying them and challenging your boundaries.

4. **Seeding Change**: With newly gained understanding and alternative perspectives, you have

the power to challenge conventional wisdom and societal norms (Hill, 1937). Use it wisely and for the greater benefit of all, for Chaos Magick bears responsibility alongside its liberties.

In the words of renowned chaos magician Peter J. Carroll, "*Belief is an instrument that you can trade anytime you want. It is meant to enhance your life, not to imprison it*" (Carroll, 1987). Let Chaos Magick continue to be your key to access unlimited potential and manifest your desires.

Review of key points and techniques

As we wrap up this fascinating journey of exploration and self-discovery, we will relook at key techniques discussed throughout the book about how to harness the power of Chaos Magick for manifestation and personal transformation.

1. **Embracing Paradox and Uncertainty**: One of the fundamental philosophical principles of Chaos Magick is the acceptance of paradox and uncertainty (Carroll, 1987). This unique, contrarian perspective is

not something to keep at arm's length, but to tap into as a source of creative power and liberation.

2. **Visualisation and Chaos Magick**: Supercharging your desire with emotional intent and visualizing it in detail makes a significant impact on the effectiveness of manifestation (Byrne, 2006). Our practical guided visualization exercises, backed by interviews from successful practitioners, aim to help you master this technique.

3. **Sigil Creation**: First outlined by Austin Osman Spare, Sigils are a potent tool encompassing your intent into a symbolic form (Spare, 2001). The step-by-step guide provided illustrates the process of crafting your Sigil.

4. **Ritual Practices**: Rituals, ranging from simple mindfulness exercises to complex ceremonial enactments, are essential to the practice of Chaos Magick (DuQuette, 2007). By following the provided practices, you take an active step in shaping your reality.

5. **Personal Transformation**: Using the principles of Chaos Magick and other philosophies, you've learned that change starts within (Hill, 1937). It's more than just conforming to societal norms; it's about redefining them using contrarian approaches.

Final words of encouragement and empowerment

We've journeyed together, into the turbulent yet empowering world of Chaos Magick, exploring the concept of embracing paradoxes and uncertainty, visualizing our desires, creating powerful sigils, performing transformative rituals, and redefining societal norms. The essence of this exploration lies in the immense power within you to manifest change and truly transform your reality.

Remember, the practice of Chaos Magick is not linear; it doesn't rely on conventional norms and, much like you, it's unique, personal, and defies convention (Carroll, 1987). You've been equipped with the tools and techniques to harness this rebellious, transformative energy. It's your spirit, your determination, and your courage that are your greatest assets.

As you forge ahead, remember Hill's wise words: "*The starting point of all achievement is desire*" (Hill, 1937). Fuel your desire with the untamed power of Chaos Magick, channel your intent, design profound rituals, and visualize your ideal future with laser-sharp focus. Let these practices become your compass in the whirlwind journey of manifesting change.

Let this be the beginning of your distinct narrative of personal growth and transformation. Embody the principles of Chaos Magick; create your reality, dictate your terms, break the mold, and redefine the norms. You are an entity of immense possibilities, a vessel of creative vitality that can navigate even the most chaotic of storms and commandeer the unseen forces of the universe towards creating tangible, positive change.

In closing, Peter J. Carroll's empowering wisdom serves as a potent reminder and a rallying call: "*Magic is about change, and the ability to undergo it knowingly and manifest it willingly is the heart of the Great Work*" (Carroll, 1987). Your destiny is in your hands. Embrace it, mold it, and steer it in the direction of your desires.

Your journey has only just begun. May your path be illuminated by the brilliant light of Chaos Magick, your compass guided by your unwavering will, and your heart filled with the resolute desire to manifest greatness. Here's to your journey of *Turning Chaos Into Desire: Manifesting Change.*

Next steps in your Chaos Magick journey

As you step forward into the uncharted expanses of your journey in Chaos Magick, you'll find an array of captivating discoveries awaiting you. This mystical journey is as boundless as your imagination, governed by both your determined will and turbulent, transformative chaos (Schulke, 2020).

One potent strategy in further immersing yourself in this audacious exploration is to connect with like-minded souls, those who are also deeply drawn towards the transformative power of Chaos Magick. There are myriad online forums and communities teeming with individuals who share your passion. Connect, collaborate, and share your experiences to enrich your journey further.

Empirical literature can also be of immense value. Books such as Carroll's 'Liber Null & Psychonaut' or Sherwin's 'The Book of Results' provide profound insights into the theoretical and practical aspects of Chaos Magick, connecting you to the foundational works of successful practitioners (Carroll, 1987; Sherwin, 1978). These resources offer invaluable direction as you navigate the vast world of Chaos Magick.

Moreover, practical application is key in mastering Chaos Magick. Incorporate manifestation rituals into your daily regimen. Practice your sigil creation and visualization techniques. Test and tweak. Every day and every instance serves as both a new challenge and a remarkable opportunity for growth as you manifest your desires (Hine, 1995).

Lastly, remember to remain open and adaptable. Chaos Magick is fluid and wildly undefined. Embrace the chaos, adapt to changes, and emerge stronger.

Each of these steps, taken individually or in conjunction, will serve as a potent catalyst for your journey into the heart of Chaos Magick, empowering you to master its untamed, transformative energy and employ it in manifesting positive, tangible change in your life (Greer, 2017).

References

- Carroll, Peter J. (1987). Liber Null & Psychonaut. York Beach, ME: Samuel Weiser.

- Greer, John Michael. (2017). Circles of Power: Ritual Magic in the Western Tradition. Woodbury, MN: Llewellyn Publications.

- Hine, Phil. (1995). Condensed Chaos: An Introduction to Chaos Magic. Tempe, AZ: New Falcon Publications.

- Schulke, Daniel. (2020). The Holy Book of Thoth: The Conciliation and Conquest of Creation. Richmond Vista, CA: Three Hands Press.

- Sherwin, Ray. (1978). The Book of Results. London: Revelations.

APPENDIX
Additional Reading

This book serves as your steadfast guide in unveiling and maneuvering the mysterious realms of Chaos Magick. But the journey doesn't end here; in fact, it's just the curtain-raiser of your vibrant voyage. For the knowledge-hungry and the steadfast explorers of the mystic, here are some estimable works of literature that offer more profound insights into Chaos

TURNING CHAOS INTO DESIRE

Magick, manifestation, personal transformation, and empowerment.

1. 'Liber Null & Psychonaut' by Peter J. Carroll: Widely seen as the definitive incipient text for Chaos Magick, Carroll's work brims with potent knowledge, providing the theoretical groundwork vital for a chaos magician (Carroll, 1987).

2. 'The Book of Results' by Ray Sherwin: An enricher and enhancer to practitioners of Chaos Magick, this book offers fresh dimensions to the practice and theory of magic, specifically focusing on effects and results (Sherwin, 1978).

3. 'Condensed Chaos: An Introduction to Chaos Magic' by Phil Hine: With its approachable style, it serves to demystify Chaos Magick for beginners while providing valuable insights and techniques for practitioners (Hine, 1995).

4. 'Six Ways: Approaches & Entries for Practical Magic' by Aidan Wachter: A simplicity-drenched guide that broadens your

perspectives on ritual magic. It captures the essence of understanding and applying Chaos Magick in an everyday environment (Wachter, 2018).

5. 'The Secret' by Rhonda Byrne & 'Think and Grow Rich' by Napoleon Hill: Although not strictly about Chaos Magick, these books underscore the power of thought, belief, and manifestation in shaping our reality (Byrne, 2006; Hill, 1937).

6. 'Mindset: The New Psychology of Success' by Carol S. Dweck: This book offers fresh perspectives on the impact mindset can have on our professional and personal lives, empowering the reader for perpetual growth (Dweck, 2006).

The aforementioned books, each noteworthy in their respective spheres, can be the stepping stones in diversifying and deepening your understanding of chaos, manifestation, and personal transformation.

Further resources for study, application and practice of Chaos Magick principles

Here are some additional resources to ensure a more comprehensive grasp and practical application of the principles of Chaos Magick.

1. Online Chaos Magick Course by Magick.Me: This online course delivers a compact and comprehensive curriculum for practitioners of all levels, providing a step by step guide to Chaos Magick (Starr, 2021).

2. 'Chaos Matrix': A vast online repository showcasing diverse writings, rituals and practices specific to Chaos Magick (Random, 1995).

3. Digital Chaos Magick Forum: An interactive platform allowing aspiring magicians to exchange ideas, experiences, and queries related to their magick journey (Reddit, 2022).

4. 'Chaotopia!: Sorcery and Ecstasy in the Fifth Aeon' by Dave Lee: Lee explores the dynamic and

transformative intersection of Chaos Magick and ecstasy, challenging conventional mindsets (Lee, 2006).

5. 'Reality Transurfing: Steps I-V' by Vadim Zeland: Although not explicitly about Magick, this series highlights principles closely connected to the idea of shaping reality, directly benefiting those practicing Chaos Magick (Zeland, 2004).

6. 'Hands-On Chaos Magic: Reality Manipulation Through the Ovayki Current' by Andrieh Vitimus: This book provides practical exercises, allowing readers to experience the power of Chaos Magick directly (Vitimus, 2009).

7. Podcast: 'Runesoup': A podcast by Gordon White that covers topics like magic, mythology, and mysticism. Subscribe and immerse yourself in the unexpected intersections between these realms (White, 2020).

Each resource mentioned ensures you gain a more profound understanding of Chaos Magick, its application, and how to practice within your daily life.

AUTHOR BIO

Orion Myst is a seasoned author and experienced tech professional, recognized for a unique narrative style that seamlessly integrates the often divergent worlds of technology, meditation, and psychedelics. Orion creates a new paradigm of thought within his works, effortlessly bridging the gap between ancient wisdom and modern realities.

His broad spectrum of interests, ranging from mind exploration to EDM/Trance festivals, enhances the richness and relevance of his writing. By combining his love for meditation and psychedelics with his professional background in technology, Orion produces thought-provoking insights that empower readers towards personal growth and transformation.

Having already acclaimed four successful titles to his name, Orion now presents his fifth work, *Turning Chaos Into Desire: Manifesting Change*. His other notable publications include *Higher Wisdom: Insights from Ancient Masters to Modern Minds*, exploring how ancient teachings can be applied to contemporary life; *Conscious Connections: Hosting MDMA Gathering*', delving into conscious party culture; *Beyond the Ordinary: Psychedelics in Professional Life*, providing a unique exploration of psychedelics in professional development, and *Designing Serenity: The Transformative Power of Home*' where interior design meets holistic living.

But at the heart of it all, Orion doesn't lose sight of what truly matters. His connection with his wife,

Wendy, and their children, Skylar and Cameron, is his primary source of inspiration. Reserving his free time for quality moments with his family and immersion into nature, Orion cultivates a harmonious balance, a manifested reality that mirrors the empowering principles he espouses in his works.

Combining the mastery of a tech professional with the wisdom of a seasoned author, Orion Myst hosts a transformative journey for readers, enriching minds and expanding horizons. With his unique approach, Orion fosters a remarkable space of dialogue within his books, ushering in a revolutionary wave in the realm of personal growth and spirituality. Drawing up the blueprint for an enlightened, fulfilled life, he is a guiding light helping others navigate the path of personal transformation.